Come unto Me, All Ye That Labor and Are Heavy Laden, and *I Will Give You Rest*

The Reality of the Holy Spirit and the Power of Prayer and Fasting as Proven by the Author

Navlet C. Linton

WESTBOW PRESS
A DIVISION OF THOMAS NELSON
& ZONDERVAN

WestBow Press books may be ordered through booksellers or by contacting:

WestBow Press
A Division of Thomas Nelson & Zondervan
1663 Liberty Drive
Bloomington, IN 47403
www.westbowpress.com
844-714-3454

Scripture taken from the King James Version of the Bible.

ISBN: 978-1-6642-2403-2 (sc)
ISBN: 978-1-6642-2404-9 (e)

Library of Congress Control Number: 2021903326

Print information available on the last page.

WestBow Press rev. date: 03/16/2021

This book is dexicated to the following persons:
Lilian McGrath, my grandmother
Morrace N. Tomlinson, my son
Selvin Linton, my father
Jahmiel Jacquet, my daughter

Contents

Preface

About five years ago, I thought of sharing my spiritual experiences and the miracles experienced after prayer and meditation and sometimes fasting, but I did not know how to start. I once made a rough draft, which I lost. These thoughts keep coming back to me.

I woke up one morning in September 2020, and the thoughts just flowed in my head. I thought, *Wow! Why didn't I think this way before?* As a result, I started to write immediately, as the memories kept on flowing. Within three days, I completed a rough draft and started to reread and edit it. I was still unsure about the topic and format, but every day that I prayed for guidance, I came up with better and better wording. I later pondered how to format the writing and decide what title I should use. It was a haphazard project at first, but everything fell in place later.

Between the ages of eleven and twelve, I had an incredibly unique experience that never left my mind. I kept it a secret for approximately fifty-four years. The memory of this experience impacted my entire life and influenced my decision to get baptized and serve the lord fully, which happened on March 31, 1991.

Growing up, I had plenty of everything—food, nice clothes to wear (socks and ribbons to match), and so forth—but the emotional aspect was zero. When I was older, I asked permission to allow school friends to spend time with me, so it was a little better than when I was younger. My grandmother meant well and taught me morals; I knew she cared very much. We attended church every Sunday. However, she did not know about emotional needs such as spending quality time with a child and how to respond to the cries for attention from a child. She just did not learn these things. She never knew the value or importance of conversation, especially with a young child. "Children should be seen and not heard" was a common belief she practiced. The emptiness I felt was sometimes unbearable.

As for the unique experience I had as a girl, it crossed my mind after many years that I should share this experience and share my testimony of the reality of God.

I bear my testimony of the reality of God and the powers of the Holy Spirit to everyone I meet, but I have never shared personal experiences. I often wonder about my loyalty to God and why I am not given more spiritual gifts so that I can better help others, but then I remember that I have not even shared my experiences with others. The purpose of this writing is to testify that there is a God. From time to time, individuals question whether it is just an illusion or whether God is real. I did wonder too before this experience. I am defending the existence of God due to my experiences of his powers, which are available for any and every human being if they only believe and trust him with all their hearts.

Introduction

In this book, I will cover principles of the Bible with emphasis on specific instructions from Jehovah, along with scripture verses for clarity. I will also share details of my testimony, prayers, fasting, and miracles. I will share the experiences of the power of prayer and healing and how a direct link to the Creator via the Holy Spirit is possible and real. It does not matter what the problem is, be it sickness, disability, homelessness, or loneliness—he is capable of healing and comforting.

Emphasis will be placed on the reality of God and how important it is to obey his words. How secure and confident one can feel in his arms even in times of pandemics and disasters.

God is the same yesterday, today, and forever; he still heals the sick and raises the dead.

Faked Suicide

I felt so alone that one day between eleven and twelve years of age, I faked suicide. The sole intention was to seek attention. To this day, no one knows it was faked because no one ever asked me about it. It was after this incident that I had a unique experience.

The Vision

The following scriptures speak of visions:

"And the Lord Answered me and said, write the vision, and make it plain upon tables, that he may run that readeth it" (Hab. 2:2 KJV).

"Then spoke the Lord to Paul in the night by a vision, be not afraid, but speak, and hold not thy peace" (Acts 18:9 KJV).

Subsequent to the faked suicide incident one night after prayer fifty-four years ago, I went to bed and saw a vision. I was walking on the road alone, and suddenly I saw and felt rays of bright light shining down on me. There was a voice behind the lights. The voice said these words very clearly: "Come unto me, all ye that labor and are heavy laden, and I will give you rest" (Matthew 11:28). I have never shared this information until now, as I now feel compelled to do so. This writing is about the reality of the Creator of the universe. The more I thought about it, the more convinced I was that it was a vision.

I believe that in these last days, when so many do not believe, that Jehovah wants all persons who have testimonies of his existence to share and help others to come unto him and be saved. This is in keeping with the scripture that says when you have been warned, you should warn your brothers and sisters. I believe that if I do not write this and appeal to the hearts of the unbelievers, God will not be pleased with me. As with Job, this is what he is waiting on, for him to release my blessings.

Why Church?

Church should be a place where the spiritually weak and the strong come together and strengthen each other. It should also be a place to facilitate spiritual growth.

However, believing and knowing is not enough. Actions are needed when challenges and difficulties arise. The faith that is spoken of should be our rock. A person who believes there is a Supreme Being who is capable of taking care of his/her life that was handed over to him the day of acceptance and then baptism should understand that there is no need to worry so much to invite sickness and death. As humans, we feel concern and discomfort when certain things happen, such as sickness or loss of a job. If I say that I don't feel these things, I would be lying, but to worry so much to the point of sickness is disrespectful and disloyal to the same God who is in charge. This is the kind of trust he expects and deserves. Patience is a virtue, pray and be patient.

Put yourself in the Creator's place for a minute. Suppose you are given a job and a job description, but at the same time, the person who entrusted you with this job kept worrying, watching over you, and calling you. How would you feel?

The Bible said to do onto others as you would have them do unto you. If you cannot trust the person you call God, why do you expect him to trust you? Can he trust you to love one another as he has loved you? Can he trust you to do unto others as you would have them do unto you?

Knowledge of What God Said

You are my friends if you do what I command (John 15:14 KJV).

I am of the feeling that many people depend on preachers to tell them what is in the Bible. They read what was addressed in church that week or that day, but what about the entire Bible? Why should we limit ourselves when there is so much to learn? It is by searching the scripture that a friendship can be developed with God.

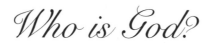

Who is God?

"I am the way, the truth, and the life; no man cometh unto the father but by me" (John 14:6).

God is like a key that you use to drive a vehicle. He can take you anywhere, but without the key, you cannot move—so get that key.

God is like the things that are immensely powerful but cannot be seen by the physical eyes. For example, the wind is felt, but can it be seen? Pain is felt, but can it be seen? Fear is very powerful, but can we see fear?

Anyone can get close to God by searching the scriptures and doing his will. God wants to be our friend. If we search with all our hearts, he will be found (Prov. 2:1–5).

He can choose to appear in the flesh, but he uses people by allowing the spirit to speak through them even if they are not aware. The Bible says "he that hath an ear let him hear what the spirit saith unto the churches" (see Rev. 2:29; Matt. 11:15.) When someone is blessed with spiritual eyes, he or she sees more than the natural man does. One of the gifts of Jehovah is spiritual eyes via the Holy Spirit to lead and guide always.

The following topics are important, as stated in the Holy Bible:

Humility

I will tell you how people who are not humble behave. They do not listen to understand, and some do not listen at all; if they do listen, they only listen to certain people, not all people. Research has shown that humble people handle stress better and benefit from higher levels of physical and mental well-being. Humility is also great for relationships, especially with God. Without humility, it is difficult to experience God, hear his answers, or recognize his work.

Friendship with God

Friendship with Jehovah follows similar principle as friendship with man. It requires getting to know the person. The difference is that man does not necessarily have any particular rules to obey as Jehovah does. Getting to know man means frequent meetings and conversations. On the other getting to know Jehovah means frequent reading of his words and prayer and fasting.

"And the scripture was fulfilled that says Abraham believed God and it was imputed to him for righteousness—and he was called the friend of God" (James 2:23).

"Ye adulterer and adulteresses, know ye not that the friendship of the world is in enmity with God? whosoever therefore will be a friend of the world is the enemy of God" (James 4:4).

Prayers

It is via prayer that we communicate with God, and it is via his scriptures that he speaks to us. He always answers prayers, but not all hear or see, for it requires humility to be able to discern the answer. God appears daily, but only the humble will recognize his presence because he is a spirit who works through humans or animals.

"And the Lord open the mouth of the ass, and she said unto Balaam, what have I done unto thee that thou hast smitten me these three times?" (Num. 22:28)

"Judas said unto him, not Iscariot, lord, how is it that thou will manifest thyself unto us, and not unto the world? Jesus answered and said unto him, if a man loves me, he will keep my words and my father will love him, and we will come unto him and make our abode with him" (John 14:22).

I testify to you that prayer works and God answers (Mark 11:24).

My adopted daughter was securely bonded to me, and when we had to be separated, she had bad experiences at a young age, which necessitated relocation repeatedly. It was exceedingly difficult to find someone who would treat her as their own child, even with pay. Her experiences were very traumatic.

She later, developed seizures, and it was discovered that there was something the size of a marble in her brain. Doctors believed our separation contributed even though there were other factors. This was my third bad experience: a family member had died tragically; my grandmother who mothered me fell and broke her hip; all tragedies occurred after I migrated. Like Job, I did not curse God and die. Instead, I prayed more and cried to God every morning and every night for strength and preservation of my sanity.

For the seizure, she had to get injections every three months, which is costly. I was not only taking care of her but also my grandmother, who required help twenty-four seven. I could not save, but I was contented that I could take care of them.

Her education was interrupted. She needed surgery, which scared both of us. I told her that God would heal her; no surgery would be necessary because the God I serve would remove it, working through the doctor. I started to ask God to intervene by having mercy on us both. I was uncomfortable but not to the point of sickness or break down because deep down I feel strongly that Jehovah will intervene.

She was admitted to the hospital, and a doctor took great interest in the case. He worked very hard on her case via research and consultation. Eventually certain medications were identified and they showed positive signs of having a strong effect. Up to the time of writing, the process is still ongoing, but I know without a doubt that God is working on the case. I would lie if I say I feel comfortable but my faith make me whole. Every time I started to think, I prayed or cried to God. I asked him to free me of this burden.

My daughter said, "Mommy, you told me long ago that God is going to work through the doctor." The doctor said he had never tried that method before.

I was not alone in prayer; I gave her name to many followers of Christ.

I lost my job for reasons still unknown to me. This was the first tragedy; the others came after. To be honest I cant explain how am still sane or alive. I was so stressed I could not concentrate. I started to ask Jehovah please don't let me lose my sanity.

I fasted for three days. After that, I went on Craigslist, and the first job I responded to called me later. I went with confidence and faith. It was such a good interview; I was not asked for anything until after I started working. My financial obligations in my country were hanging around my neck. When I cried and prayed, I reminded God of the persons who depended on me, including children. I worked at that job for one year. Things were still not working out.

I went on Craiglist again and landed a live-in job in another state. as I had no one to stay with. After six weeks I got no pay. I met someone on the job who was experiencing the same problem, and she asked her friend to help me with accommodations, with the hope of another job soon so I could help her financially.

After three months of trying daily, no job was forthcoming because everyone needed retraining. The woman I stayed with was aware of my efforts. She commented that she had never met anyone who had tried so hard. I even studied and passed the insurance examination to be a salesperson. I took care of the household chores and helped her as much as I could. I went every morning to a church for breakfast and for dinner in the afternoon. I tried not to be a burden.

Prior to passing the exam, I noticed my housemate acting out because I had not started working. I was glad to tell her I had passed the examination. I also crocheted warm beanies for her to sell at work.

After I passed examination I needed money, to pay for things to start doing business. I prayed and asked God to help me to get at least the exact amount of dollars needed (I don't remember the figure).

One morning I was lying on the bed and went into deep meditation; I tried to focus on the Creator. I was there for about an hour when the phone rang. It was a friend from my home country. She said, "What is your address?" I was shocked and asked why she wanted to know. She replied, "I was lying in my room when you came up so strong in my mind in a way I could not ignore, so I decided to send you this amount of money." (Again, I don't remember the precise figure, but I know it was exactly what I needed at the time.)

Then I proceeded to tell her what I was doing when she called and what the need was. She was happy to be a part of that special experience. The strange thing is that I had not spoken to her about the matter. In fact, we had not spoken for a long time, but she knew things were not going right since I arrived in the country.

About a week later, my housemate came to the area where I slept and expressed her disgust that I was not yet working. Then she went back to her room. I spoke to the heavenly Father as if he were sitting beside me. I said, "Did you hear that? Do you think that was fair? Please intervene, as I don't want to be here another day." Then I prayed and started to sing the lyrics to my favorite song when I am in trouble: "On the solid rock I stand; all other grounds are sinking sand."

About two hours after, my phone rang. It was about a job. They said to stand by because the man would be discharged from rehab soon. I shouted, "Thank you, Jesus!"

As soon as I got the call to start work, I went and rented storage space. I took a taxi with my things to storage in the afternoon and started the next day. The entire family received me so well.

After the client died, I had no place to go. I did not tell any of them, but they knew I had just arrived from another state; they also knew that I'd worked six weeks and was not paid. One day the wife, who had become a widow, said to me, "You can stay here as long as you want to." I was amazed. I lived there and was treated as a family member for one year and three months. Then I went on my own. Jehovah can use anyone to do whatever he wants them to do.

Obedience

We disobeyed from time to time and did not view it as any big thing. How do we feel when our children outrightly disobey us? (See Exod. 23:25 KJV)

Hate

I do not know how it feels to hate someone. I've felt disgusted and angered, but hate is too strong and should not be entertained. I cannot remember if I felt that emotion when I was younger—maybe I did. Ever since I read in the Bible what God said about hate, I replace the strong feeling of disgust with sympathy for the people who willfully offend me. Hate does not make sense, and it is something that the distorted mind resorts to.

"Whosoever hateth his brother is a murder and ye know that no murderer hath eternal life abiding in him "(1 John 3:15).

You will notice that it did not give exceptions. For example, it did not say except the murderer, or the homosexuals, or the person of a different race. Our prejudices originate from our socialization. It is possible to ignore what was learned as a child, be it good or bad. People do it every day, but unfortunately, they seem to ignore the good teaching and grasp the bad more easily than the other way around. We do not have to agree, but we need to treat our brothers and sisters as human beings. God does not need help dealing with the ones we think are committing dangerous sins. In the sight of Jehovah sin is sin and they all represent disobedience to him. For example, Adultery, fornication, and homosexuality are all sexual sins. Nevertheless, while I hate the sin, I love the sinners.

Contradiction

If someone who prays every day, reads the Bible as often as possible, and goes to church weekly yet that same person when face with problems look outside realm of God for solution. What does this mean? Do some people view God the same way they view Santa Claus? In those persons' minds, is God a reality or an illusion? Or is he too slow in their minds and they want something quicker. I mention this because many persons seem to be always in a rush even when there is no need to be.

Love and Respect

Like bacon and eggs, these two go hand in hand. If we love God, we want to please him and keep his commandments (see John 14:15 KJV), not because we desire to do so but because God asked us to do so. It is as plain and simple as that.

God has minutely shown his care to us: clean air, food, water, shelter, beautiful plants and flowers; many mysteries which we cant understand. For example the making of honey by bees.; and many more. What happens if all the crops stop growing?; the sun stop shining or the rain stop falling.?

What happens if God starts to think like man in terms of punishment? We know he will not think like that even when he is angry as he is now! He is a merciful God, and he gives time for repentance and change. God does not judge as man does; he looks at the heart, not the outward appearance. God does not judge as man does: "But the Lord said unto Samuel *look not on his countenance or the height of his stature because I have refused him........*" (1 Sam. 16:7 KJV).

How do we prove to God that we respect him and care about his instructions? It's simple - We obey.

Man is not always able to fix problems by himself. Whatever is keeping him from a relationship with the heavenly Father should be addressed via prayer, fasting, and, if necessary, professional help, but we must seek ye first the kingdom of God and his righteousness and experience the addition of all the things he promises (Isa. 65:13; Deut. 30:15).

Who Does Man Worship in Place of God?

"Thou shalt have no other God before me." It has always been my opinion that material things are overemphasized. Everyone needs money to survive, and material things add to comfort. However, material things are limited and do not guarantee peace of mind and happiness. Many believe money and material possession are the be-all and end-all, but after they've achieved everything and have lots of money, they become so disappointed. Some people even give away the material things because they feel they brought them more unhappiness and loneliness.

The most important things in life are not always things that can be bought; in other words love on the basis of money, has a shorter life. On the other hand true love is unconditional and is everlasting.

For example, a woman in love loves only one man, and the same goes for the man. What a person feels in the heart manifest in a unique way, and the difference is conspicuous to those who are observant.

How many persons would stop to pick up an injured person and take him/her to hospital? I don't believe many would. Most people are more concerned about the mess of a car than the life of another human being. A car can be washed or replaced, but a life cannot be replaced. Once it is gone, it is over. So not only has man worshipped material things, but he has also shown that they are more important than life. It is not money that is the root of all evil. It is the attitude toward money, the constant obsession, and preoccupation of money thoughts mainly by those who don't have it and desire to be rich.

Lies/Truth

Lies are like darkness and represents the devil. On the other hand light and truth represent Jehovah. Each time a lie is told the person without realizing has chosen a side. If this becomes a habit not to speak truth after a while there will be confusion to the point that its difficult for the individual to differentiate between the two.

Testimony

For I am not ashamed of the gospel because it is the power of God that brings salvation to everyone who believes, first to the Jew then to the Gentiles (Rom. 1:16 KJV).

The testimonies I have of God's powers are numerous and striking. God is not an illusion; he is alive, active, and willing to be there for anyone and everyone. He wants to be our friend.

I did everything alone, even travel to foreign countries, without any kind of human support. Even though it appeared that I was alone, I never walk alone. God seems to look out for persons like myself; otherwise, what would have happened to us?

And ye shall seek me and find me when he shall search with all thy heart (Jer. 29:13 KJV).

I was at the edge of a cliff, but he pulled me back. Every crossroads my life experienced, someone appeared from I do not know where to rescue or guide me without asking for pay. Every single time I was lost or got into what appeared to be deep danger, an angel appeared.

If I am tired and am about to oversleep, there is someone to wake me up. All my life, every time I am confused and have no one to have discussions with, all I do is pray before I go to sleep. As soon as I wake in the morning, the first thing to my mind is the answer (Haggai 1:13 KJV; Prov. 3:5-6; Mathew 7:7-11; James 1:5-6).

When they read this book, many persons will ask, "Why should I turn over my life and give up all the things I enjoy [which may not be of God but about fun]." They will say, "What did I achieve? I am still working at retirement age. I am not rich."

Let me explain what and why:

I am overweight but enjoy perfect health at my age. I sleep eight hours a night. I am not perfect regarding dieting, but still I am healthy. I have faced numerous persecutions, including homelessness and joblessness in a foreign place, without any relatives or friends, just myself among strangers. To date, I have no mental issues, and I have not gone to any professional, nor have I crossed any lines. I remain sane, and my blood pressure is normal. Do you believe these blessings are just coincidental or that I am special?

I am just an ordinary person from a humble background who has decided to put God first and to rely on prayer and fasting. This has worked, so I don't have to be rich in materials. I am rich in the spirit; I feel so free and protected, regardless of what is happening around me. This is what I want everyone to feel. It is a long and challenging journey but a rewarding one.

My life—every minute, hour, day, week, month, and year—is based on prayer. I pray about every problem, every challenge, every decision, and I wait for guidance. Sometimes guidance comes to me at the last minute. My eyes opened to the con artists who appeared real, and I started to see things I had overlooked. I have been saved numerous times from conmanship, especially online.

I worked at a job for one year, and every day a trap was set for me in order to get me fired. I was not aware of these things, but every time I reported to work and saw something strange, I corrected it or sought clarity. I am usually a detailed person, but if it were not for God's spirit, I could not have seen some of the things because they were not that obvious. When nothing worked, they had to lie to get me fired, and the officer came to the location I was assigned, to inform me about the decision. She first looked at me and said, "You are a very intelligent person." I was puzzled but after careful thinking and reviewing I realized that all the strange things were not coincident but rather trap. When everything failed they lied. The Officer knew about the plots that's why she made the comment. Even though am a detailed person I just on my own could not noticed all. I firmly believe it was divine.

Prayer worked for me, and it can work for anyone. These are my testimonies of a supreme power. I gave God total respect, when I prayed, I do not tell him what to do; I asked. I love my neighbor. I do good to enemies. I try to obey him and do what he said. Even in my imperfections, I still try. It is not about perfection or sinlessness; it is the lack of respect for him. In other words, willful continuous sin without regard for his feelings and instructions. When I am tempted to do wrong, I first think of how I will feel when I kneel to pray. Just the feeling of disloyalty and dishonesty are enough to stop me or bring discomfort.

In the sight of God, every human being is important. Judgment is the business of God. He said- "But the very hairs of your head are all numbered" (Matt. 10:30).

The following song lyrics are what I sing, especially in times of trials. They seem to have not just comfort but also powers:

Song Lyrics

My hope is built on nothing less than Jesus christ, my righteousness; I dare not trust the sweetest frame, but wholly lean on Jesus name.

1) On Christ, the solid rock, I stand; all other ground is sinking sand, all other ground is sinking sand,

2) When darkness veils his lovely face, I rest on his unchanging grace; in every high and stormy gale, my anchor holds within the veil. His oath, his covenant, his blood, supports me in the whelming flood; when all around my soul gives way, He then is all my hope and stay.

    I do not worry about tomorrow I just live from day to day because I know who holds tomorrow and I know who holds my hand.

"Give a man a dollar and you cheer his heart; give him a dream and you challenge his heart; give him Christ and you change his heart." —C. Neil Strait

Reference

Holy Bible King James Version
C. Neil Strait
Quote – give a man a dollar...."

Printed in the United States
by Baker & Taylor Publisher Services